CW00432263

1

An English Easter

Part of the GRANNY HOOPER™ series

Sarah Studholme

An English Easter, Sarah Studholme

Contents:

Introduction:

I live near London with my husband and two daughters. It is quite an international area, so there are many families with different cultures and family traditions. We are seen to be a typical English family and I find that I am often asked what the "typically English way" to do something is, or for a "typically English recipe" for a certain occasion.

I realised that, whilst there are many recipe books filled with numerous dishes that can be prepared for events throughout the year, such as Christmas and Easter, there are very few, if any, that really apply these recipes or craft activities in the context for which they were intended.

My grandmother taught me many of the recipes and traditions that I cover in my books, so she is very much the inspiration behind them. It therefore felt natural to create the "Granny Hooper" brand, and "An English Easter" is one of the books in the series.

Granny Hooper was born in England in 1923 and in her late teens studied at one of the country's leading Schools of Cookery. Several of the recipes included in this book are her modified versions of recipes acquired from her time at the school. Granny Hooper was a model student and stayed on after graduating to become a teaching assistant. Her skills were not only limited to cooking and baking, she was also excellent at traditional crafts such as dressmaking, needlepoint, knitting and flower arranging.

With three daughters, seven grandchildren and three great-grandchildren when she died in 2013, Granny Hooper was able to see her enthusiasm and skills in cookery and crafts being passed down the generations.

I hope that by sharing the traditional recipes and craft ideas that have become core family traditions in our household, this book will help to explain why they are carried out and how you can enjoy creating them too.

Chapter 1, Lent:

Shrove Tuesday and Pancakes

Shrove Tuesday is the day before Ash Wednesday in the Christian calendar. It is named after the ritual of shriving, which is when people used to confess their sins and receive forgiveness for them before the start of Lent on Ash Wednesday.

Lent was traditionally a time for fasting when Pope St Gregory forbid the consumption of meat and animal products. This included butter, eggs and milk. People tried to use up these items before the start of Lent and a recipe combining them was devised called pancakes.

Tradition:

It has become a British tradition to eat pancakes on Shrove Tuesday. In fact, it is so popular that the day is commonly known as Pancake Day instead of Shrove Tuesday.

Granny Hooper's Pancake recipe:

Makes 8 thin crepe-style pancakes

15 minutes to make the batter, 3 minutes to cook each pancake

Ingredients	Equipment
Batter: • 110g plain flour • 1 egg • 290ml milk • 15g salted butter melted • 10g salted butter to grease pan To serve: • 2 lemons cut in quarters • 30g granulated sugar	• Sieve • Medium sized bowl • Electric whisk or balloon whisk • Weighing scales • Measuring jug if scales don't measure liquids • Frying pan • Ladle • Knife • Wooden spoon • Palette knife • Hob • Kitchen paper towel

Granny Hooper Tip:

The batter is better if it is allowed to rest for a few hours before serving. If possible, make the batter earlier in the day and cook later, just before you are wanting to eat the pancakes.

1. Sift the flour into the bowl and make a hole in the centre with the spoon, otherwise known as a well.

2. Break the egg in the well and pour in approximately 50ml of the milk and stir the liquid to mix the egg and milk together.

3. Gradually draw more flour from the edges of the well into the liquid and stir so that it is smooth with no lumps.

4. Add more milk as the liquid in the bowl thickens and repeat until all the flour has been combined.

5. Pour in any remaining milk and add the melted butter.

6. Now switch to the electric whisk or balloon whisk. Whisk the mixture for about 1 minute if using the electric whisk or 5 minutes if using the balloon whisk. The liquid should be a thick, smooth, bubbly batter with the consistency of cream.

7. If possible, leave the batter to rest in the fridge for a few hours and whisk again just before cooking.

8. Place the frying pan on the hob and heat it up. Drop about 3-4 grams of the butter into the pan and swirl it around the pan until it coats the base. It should be sizzling hot.

9. Now pour 1 ladle of the batter into the pan and tilt the pan so that the batter covers the base in a thin layer.

10. As the pancake cooks on the high heat, you will see bubbles forming and the batter starting to go solid with just a slight dampness left on top. Use the palette knife to lift a corner of the pancake. It should be a light, golden colour underneath and move freely if you wobble the pan. It is now time to cook the other side.

11. If you are feeling brave, flip the pancake by removing the pan from the heat and flipping it upwards so that the pancake rises into the air and flips over. Catch the pancake in the pan and return it to the heat. If you are worried about doing this, you can place the palette knife under the pancake and flip it over that way.

12. Cook the second side of the pancake for about a minute on the high heat and then check the colour on the bottom of the pancake by lifting it with the palette knife. If it is golden, it is ready to serve.

13. To cook the next pancake, use the kitchen paper towel to remove any brown residue from the base of the pan and return the pan to the high heat.

14. Drop in another very small piece of butter to re-grease the pan and repeat steps 9. to 12.

15. When eating the pancake, it should be placed flat on a plate and sprinkled with a small spoonful of the sugar. Now squeeze the juice from one of the lemon quarters over the sugar and roll the pancake up into a long cylinder shape.

When making pancakes, you are always unlucky if you are chosen as the chef! As a child I remember my mother cooking our pancakes and each family member would queue up to receive theirs. They were so delicious that you would quickly devour your pancake and then race back to queue up for your next one. The result would be that the poor chef would spend the evening over the hot stove flipping pancakes that everyone else would enjoy. The chef would only get a few moments to quickly consume their pancakes whilst continuing to cook the rest for everybody else!

Alternative toppings:

I have given the traditional pancake topping eaten in our family, but there are numerous delicious sweet and savoury alternatives such as:

- Maple syrup
- Bacon and maple syrup
- Greek yoghurt and summer berries
- A hot sauce made from Cointreau and melted marmalade
- Coconut yoghurt, honey and sunflower seeds
- Small chunks of ham and grated cheddar cheese
- Caramelised onion jam, grated cheddar cheese and chopped chives.

Tradition:

It is believed that sometime in the 1400s, a housewife was so busy making pancakes that she almost forgot to go to her church service. She heard the church bells ringing, so left the house and ran to church still carrying her frying pan and pancake. This tale was then turned into a traditional pancake race in some areas of England. Participants must run a certain distance whilst carrying a frying pan containing a pancake. The pancake must be tossed at the start and end of the race.

Ash Wednesday and Lent

As mentioned earlier, Ash Wednesday is the first day of Lent in the Christian calendar. Lent being the 40 days (excluding Sundays) leading up to Easter Day. The date of Easter changes every year and therefore so do Shrove Tuesday and Ash Wednesday.

Easter Sunday is the first Sunday after the full moon of the Spring equinox. The earliest date Easter could fall is 22nd March and the latest date is 25th April. As a result, Shrove Tuesday usually falls between mid-February to mid-March.

Tradition:

The name Ash Wednesday comes from the tradition of Christians going to church on this day to make a final confession of their sins at the start of Lent. The vicar or priest will draw the shape of a cross on the forehead of the worshipper in ash to symbolise their sins and also death. From this day until Easter Day, the worshipper should fast to imitate Jesus fasting in the wilderness and resisting temptations.

Nowadays, this act of fasting is represented by people giving up something that they like during Lent. It is often food related, such as giving up eating chocolate, sweets, cakes or stopping drinking alcohol, but some people decide to interpret this as a time to do something positive such as voluntary work for their local community, or fund-raising for a charity.

Chapter 2, Easter Craft:

Decorated Eggs

These eggs make beautiful Easter decorations and they are so versatile. They can be used as part of a display on your Easter table or to hang on your Easter tree.

Takes about ½ hour per egg (preparation and painting)

Materials
• Eggs – however many you want to decorate
• Kitchen skewer
• Two small bowls
• Acrylic paints for a bold strong colour with a sheen or watercolour for a more subtle colour and matt finish. Please note that watercolour will wash off if wet.
• Paintbrush
• Water in water pot
• Cleaning cloth
• Washing up liquid
• Kitchen paper towel
• Egg cups – the same number as the number of eggs

1. Take an egg and using the skewer start to tap repeatedly at the top of the egg until you feel the shell starting to weaken slightly and a small hole forming. Tap in the centre of this hole until the skewer can slide in and out.

2. Turn the egg over and repeat step 1. at the bottom of the egg.

3. Using the skewer, push it through one of the holes until it is in the centre of the egg. Move it around until you think it has pierced the yolk.

4. Take the cleaning cloth and wet it with some water. Wipe the outside of the egg all over.

5. Take the egg up to your mouth and blow hard through whichever of the two holes at the top and bottom of the egg is the smallest. Make sure that the hole at the opposite end is aimed over one of the small bowls.

6. Keep blowing through the hole until you think that all the egg liquid has come out.

7. Put some washing up liquid and warm water in the second bowl and place the egg in the soapy water so that the holes are submerged and the egg fills with some of the soapy water.

8. Blow the water out of the egg and dry it with the paper towel.

9. Put the egg in the egg cup and use the paints to decorate your egg in whatever colours or designs you like. You will be able to decorate the top half of your egg and then you will need to wait for the paint to dry before turning the egg upside down in the egg cup and decorating the other half.

10. Repeat steps 1. to 9. until all your eggs are decorated.

Ideas for decoration could include:

- Painting all the eggs in different pastel shades and then using a contrasting colour to decorate a pattern such as zig-zags or dots on the outside. The zig-zags and dots could be done using a wooden cocktail stick for extra fine detail.
- Painting the eggs the colour of real bird eggs, for example in blue, beige, white etc and then decorating with the texture of the real bird egg. These textures could be recreated using a splatter

technique running your fingers through the bristles of the paintbrush to splash the paint on, or you could use a piece of sponge dipped lightly in paint to create a mottled effect.

- The eggs could be decorated to look like people or animals with hands and feet made separately out of thick paper and glued on.

Easter Wreath

Whilst Easter wreaths are not as widely used as Christmas wreaths, there are increasing numbers of Easter wreath making courses that can be attended in the run up to Easter. The ease of these workshops is that all the components are laid out for you, so you really just need to assemble them to show your own style and then your wreath is ready to display at home.

You can save on the cost of a wreath workshop by sourcing your own components and making the wreath at home.

Takes 1-2 hours

Items to buy online or foraged

- 30 – 40cm diameter willow wreath
- Wreath door hanger (if not using ribbon to attach your wreath to your door)
- Glue gun with glue sticks
- 2 metres of your choice of pastel coloured satin or gros grain ribbon 5cm / 2-inch thickness (only 1 metre if just to have a bow at the base and not using for wreath hanging)
- Natural speckled feathers for crafting about 30 (small feathers can also be foraged)
- Speckled artificial bird eggs for crafting about 10 - 15
- Artificial moss for crafting (this can be foraged)

To assemble your Easter wreath:

1. If you are not using a door wreath hanger, then tie a 1 metre length of your pastel ribbon around what will become the top centre position of your wreath so that the securing knot falls half way down the length. You should now have two lengths of around 45cm protruding from the top to secure to your front door later.

2. Tie the remaining 1 metre length of ribbon around what will become the bottom centre position of your wreath. Tie a balanced, attractive bow and cut the tails at a 45° angle to prevent fraying.

3. Now open out the moss slightly so that it is not a solid lump. Push small pieces of it under the willow frame all around the circle so that the frame is half covered with moss and half showing exposed strands of willow.

4. When you are happy with the base appearance of the wreath, take your glue gun and put a small dollop of glue on an exposed piece of willow, then stick one of the feathers onto it. Repeat this all around the wreath until there is a scattering of feathers across the ring.

5. Place slightly larger dollops of glue on the exposed willow either straight on the wood or on part of the feathers to give a layering effect. Now stick an egg on this. Repeat until several eggs have been applied around the ring.

6. Hold the wreath up and check that you have a balanced design (or that you are happy with it if you have gone for an asymmetric look). Add extra of any component if you are not initially happy, until you are pleased with your design.

7. You are now ready to hang your wreath on your front door. If you are using a door wreath hanger, you can attach the hanger to your front door and hang the wreath from it. If you have a door knocker, tie the top ribbon tightly to the door knocker. Alternatively, you will need to put a nail in your front door and tie the ribbon to the nail to hang your wreath.

Granny Hooper Tip:

To prevent your wreath from scratching your front door as the door is opened and closed, tie some soft cotton fabric to the back of the wreath frame at the bottom where it makes contact with the door.

Flower Arranging

There are so many beautiful flowers that are in season around Easter, so it really does make sense to embrace what is on offer naturally and cheer up your home with some seasonal floral displays.

If, however, you prefer to use a flower that is symbolic of Easter but not in season in England at this time of year, you could source some white lilies from your local florist. It is believed that they grew around the base of the cross that Jesus was crucified on, and have therefore been associated with purity and new life at this time of year.

Granny Hooper was a keen flower arranger always using flowers from her own garden, yet adding a few shop-bought flowers at points in the year when the garden was lacking in blooms.

Granny Hooper Tip:

Use foliage in your garden or that you have foraged to bulk out a flower arrangement. This is particularly useful if you do not have many flowers in your garden and have to buy cut stems from the florist or supermarket. Garden foliage that works well at this time of year includes short branches of: laurel, willow, bay, pittosporum, jasmine and conifer, but you can experiment with anything.

Takes around 30 minutes

Items (quantities dependent on vase size)	Equipment
• Foliage • Flowers • Water	• Secateurs • Vase / jug / glass / pot (your choice of item to arrange in)

1. Select the vessel that you want to make your arrangement in. It is helpful to think about the type of flower you will be using so that your choice is appropriate. For example, tulips tend to droop, but are quite short in length so a shorter vessel like a jug which has a supportive neck might work well. Roses have tall thin stems that can hold the flower head well, so a tall glass vase would be a good choice.

2. Once your vessel has been chosen (this will be referred to as a vase for the rest of the instructions), fill it ¾ full with fresh water.

3. Before putting anything in your vase, lay out all your foliage and flowers that you have to work with. Hold each different plant up to the vase and work out what would look a good height. You might want the flowers to be slightly taller than the foliage so that they stand out, alternatively if the foliage were willow with buds on, you might like them to be tall as a feature, and as they are thin, you would still be able to see any flowers quite easily.

4. Once the height has been decided, cut to length using the secateurs. Make the cut at a 45° angle to aid good water uptake whilst in the vase. Also note that even if the length is already correct, you should still cut some off the bottom at a 45° angle as this will help to keep the stem alive for longer.

5. Now work out where the waterline will fall on each stem when it is in the vase. Pull off any leaves on the stem that will fall under the waterline. If they are left on, they will encourage bacteria growth which will smell unpleasant and make the arrangement die quicker.

6. You are now ready to start arranging. Take the foliage first and place it in the vase stem by stem around the outer edge, but without crowding.

7. Now take some of the flowers and create a ring of these inside your ring of foliage, again without crowding. If you are using a variety of flowers, try to ensure that you have spaced these equally around the ring of foliage, for example, flower type 1 at 12 o'clock, 3 o'clock, 6 o'clock and 9 o'clock in the vase and flower type 2 half way between each of these.

8. Now go back to the foliage and place some more stems in the vase to create another ring inside the flowers.

9. Finish with two or three of the flower stems in the centre.

10. Remember that you will be viewing your arrangement from different angles, not just face on, so turn the vase around and check that it looks good all the way around. Feel free to add more foliage or blooms where any gaps appear until you are happy with how it looks.

Granny Hooper Tip:

You will need to check your flower arrangement every 1-2 days to ensure that there is plenty of water still left for the plants to drink. Top up with fresh water using a small watering can or jug as needed. It is helpful to place your vase on a small saucer or plant plate to ensure no water stains on your surfaces from top-up spillages or leaking vases.

Another tip is that an arrangement can be revived when some blooms die, by transferring the surviving blooms and foliage to a smaller vase and following stems 2. to 10. again.

Easter Cards

As a family we always send Easter cards to each other. It is a nice way to remind family members that you are thinking of them and also provides them with some seasonal decoration in their home. It is nice to send the card a couple of weeks before Easter Day so that it can be received and enjoyed for the full Holy Week, which runs from Palm Sunday through to Easter Day.

Palm Sunday is the Sunday before Easter Sunday. It is the day that Jesus arrived into Jerusalem and it is often celebrated today with processions of people, often led by a donkey, carrying palm branches.

The cards that we send at this time of year can be purchased. They often show symbols of new life or rebirth, such as blossoming flowers, chicks hatching out of eggs or rabbits. Equally they may focus on the more commercial side of Easter and display decorated or chocolate eggs, or the Easter Bunny character who, according to folklore carries coloured eggs in a basket to the houses of young children.

Instead of buying Easter cards, you or your children might enjoy making them as a craft activity. There are numerous design ideas and video guides of how to create these on the internet.

Granny Hooper Tip:

When you take down your Easter cards after Easter, cut out the design on the front with either regular scissors or pinking shears. You can then mount this on a contrasting colour of paper or card with a 5mm border showing around the cut-out design. Now take an A5 piece of white card and fold it in half to make a greeting card shape. Stick the coloured paper with design card on it onto the folded white card. You now have a lovely recycled Easter card ready to send next Easter.

Easter Tree

A really attractive and simple decoration for your house at Easter time is an Easter tree. You can either forage for 50-100cm long branches of flowering trees such as pussy willow or cherry blossom or non-flowering trees with side branches.

Takes around 1 hour to assemble excluding time to make decorated eggs and paint branches.

Items (quantities dependent on vase size)	Equipment
• Branches as detailed above – foraged, purchased from florists or faux branches purchased from shops • Water • 7 – 10 Decorated eggs from craft activity listed earlier • 30cm lengths of pastel coloured 5-10mm wide ribbon (one length per egg, so quantity depends on number of eggs) • White paint if painting your branches	• Secateurs • Scissors • Glue gun with glue sticks • Tall Vase / jug / watering can (your choice of item to arrange in) • Paint brush if painting your branches • Newspaper if painting your branches

1. If you are painting your branches, lay some newspaper down as it can get messy! Now use the brush to paint all over the branches. Push the bristles into any bends to give a fully coated finish. Leave to dry on the newspaper.

2. Take your vase or vessel of choice to arrange you Easter Tree in. If you are using living branches, fill your vessel ½ to ¾ full with water to ensure any flowers or buds last longer, if not, leave the vessel empty.

3. Arrange your branches in the vessel so that they splay out nicely.

4. Take a length of ribbon and tie the ends together in a tight knot with about 10mm of tail remaining from each end. You should now have a big loop.

5. Place a pea sized dollop of glue on the top point of one of your decorated eggs and carefully stick the knot in the middle of this and press each of the two tails into the glue 180° apart from each other. Let the glue dry.

6. Repeat stages 4. and 5. until all eggs have hanging loops.

7. You can now hang your eggs from the branches in your vessel. Remember to place them at different heights and space them at intervals to give a balanced display.

8. Place your Easter Tree on the hearth, in the centre of your kitchen table or any other focal point where it will be admired, but won't get knocked over.

As an alternative to hanging decorated eggs, you can buy ready-made Easter tree decorations. These might be rabbits, chicks, eggs and flowers which will already be fitted with hanging loops.

Chapter 3, Easter Bakes:

Simnel Cake

Serves 11 slices (or more if not giving 1 ball per slice)

Marzipan takes 10 minutes to make, 2 hours to chill

Cake takes 20-30 minutes to make, 2½-3 hours to cook, 10 minutes to decorate when cool

Ingredients	Equipment
<ul><li>110g currants</li><li>110g sultanas</li><li>110g raisins</li><li>110g mixed chopped peel</li><li>110g glace cherries, halved</li><li>225g plain flour</li><li>225g caster sugar</li><li>1 teaspoon mixed spice</li><li>1 teaspoon ground cinnamon</li><li>225g butter</li><li>Grated rind of 2 lemon</li><li>Grated rind of 2 oranges</li><li>4 large eggs</li><li>1 tablespoon brandy</li><li>2 tablespoons sieved apricot jam</li><li>1 egg beaten to glaze at the end</li></ul> Marzipan <ul><li>500g pack marzipan</li></ul>Or <ul><li>85g caster sugar</li><li>140g icing sugar</li><li>225g ground almonds</li><li>Grated rind of 1 orange</li><li>1 egg beaten</li><li>½ teaspoon of orange juice</li></ul>	<ul><li>large mixing bowl</li><li>20cm diameter cake tin (loose bottomed is preferable)</li><li>Baking parchment or greaseproof paper</li><li>Brown paper or newspaper</li><li>String</li><li>Weighing scales</li><li>Wooden spoon</li><li>Teaspoon</li><li>Tablespoon</li><li>Metal spoon</li><li>Sieve</li><li>Grater</li><li>Juicer</li><li>Knife</li><li>Wire rack</li><li>Metal skewer</li><li>Rolling pin</li><li>Cling film or beeswax wrap if making marzipan</li><li>Fork</li><li>Pastry brush</li></ul>

Part One: Make the Marzipan if not using ready-made:

1. Put the all the ingredients in a bowl and stir together or beat in a food processor until a paste has been formed.

2. Dust a work surface with icing sugar. Scoop the almond paste out of the bowl and make it into a ball shape, then put it on the work surface.

3. Knead the ball until it becomes smooth in texture.

4. Wrap in cling film or beeswax wrap and chill in the fridge for 2 hours.

Part Two: The Simnel Cake:

1. Line the cake tin with two layers of baking parchment or greaseproof paper.

2. Make a double layer out of the brown paper or newspaper and tie it with the string around the outside of the tin to create an outer band. This will enable the cake to cook gently and insulate it.

3. Using the wooden spoon, cream the butter, sugar and citrus rinds in the mixing bowl until pale and fluffy.

4. Add the eggs one at a time beating well after each one is added.

5. Sieve the flour and spices into the mixture and use the metal spoon to fold this in carefully.

6. Add the brandy and stir until you have a smooth mixture.

7. Mix all the fruit together and add to the mixture stirring until everything is evenly combined.

8. Spoon half of the mixture into the lined cake tin using the back of the spoon to push it into the corners and smooth over the top.

9. Dust a work surface with icing sugar and roll out the marzipan until it is about 5mm thick.

10. Use the cake tin as a guide to cut out two circles from the marzipan. Keep the scraps for later.

11. Place one circle on the cake mixture in the tin and press down lightly.

12. Spoon the remaining cake mixture on top of the marzipan and use the back of the spoon to push it into the corners and smooth over the top. Give the tin a bang on the worksurface to ensure that there are no air pockets and then make a small dip in the centre.

13. Put a layer of newspaper or brown paper on the shelf in the oven and place the cake tin on top of this.

14. Bake at 150°C for 2½-3 hours.

15. After 1½ hours, place a double layer of baking parchment or greaseproof paper over the top of the cake. This will stop it from overcooking on the top.

16. After 2½ hours, use a metal skewer to test whether the cake is cooked. The skewer should come out clean. If there is residue, return the cake to the oven and check at 15-minute intervals.

17. When the cake is cooked, remove from the oven and let it cool in the tin.

18. Once cool, remove the cake from the tin and place on the wire rack to become stone-cold.

19. Spread a thin layer of apricot jam over the top of the cake and place the second marzipan circle on the top. Use the back of the fork to press around the edge of the marzipan to give a striped pattern.

20. Using the marzipan scraps, make 11 equal sized balls.

21. Use the pastry brush to brush the beaten egg over the top of the marzipan disk already on the cake.

22. Place the 11 balls equally around the top to form a ring, pressing in slightly to ensure each one is secure. Now brush the top of each ball with the remaining beaten egg.

23. Put the cake under the grill for a few seconds until the egg glaze browns slightly. Be careful as it can quickly go from brown to burnt if left too long!

24. Your cake is now ready to present on a nice cake plate or stand. It tastes lovely with a cup of Afternoon Blend tea.

Tradition:

The reason that there are 11 balls on top of the Simnel cake is that they represent Jesus' 12 disciples minus Judas. This is because Judas betrayed Jesus by disclosing where Jesus was hiding in the Garden of Gethsemane. This led to his arrest and eventually his execution.

Iced Easter Shortbreads

These biscuits, with their hint of lemon flavour, are delicious. They are quick and easy to make if they are eaten un-iced, but the full iced version does take time. The end result, however, is more than worth it. They really do look impressive and make a wonderful gift. Children will love cutting the shortbread shapes and helping with the decoration of these biscuits.

Makes about 25 medium sized shortbreads

Shortbreads take 20-30 minutes to prepare, 1 hour to chill, 10 minutes to cook

Icing takes 30-45 minutes to prepare, 30-45 minutes to decorate

Ingredients	Equipment
For biscuits: • 200g salted butter • 200g caster sugar • 400g plain flour • 1 egg lightly beaten • Grated zest of 1 lemon For icing: • 500g royal icing mix • 80ml cold water • A range of gel food colourings	• large mixing bowl • wooden spoon • weighing scales • grater • sieve • biscuit cutters in Easter shapes e.g. egg, flower, rabbit, chick, lamb • rolling pin • palette knife • wire cooling rack • non-stick baking tray • metal tablespoon • electric hand whisk • ramekin dishes or small bowls (one for each colour of line and flood icing you are making) • several teaspoons • piping bags with writing nozzle (one for each colour of line icing you are making) • squeezy icing bottles with nozzle fitted (one for each colour of flood icing you are making)

Part One: Making the biscuits:

1. Cream the butter, sugar and lemon zest in a large mixing bowl with the wooden spoon until they form a creamy mixture. Do not overwork or the biscuits will spread during baking.

2. Beat in the egg until it is combined in the mixture.

3. Switch to the metal spoon and sieve in the flour and stir until it is all combined and the mixture forms a dough.

4. Gather the mixture into a large ball and wrap in cling film or beeswax wrap, then place in the fridge to cool for at least 1 hour.

5. Place the dough on a floured surface and roll out to 5mm thickness.

6. Use the cutters to cut out the shapes and lift them with the palette knife onto the non-stick baking tray, ensuring that they are not too close together.

Granny Hooper Tip:

If you want to hang any of your biscuits from your Easter Tree, cut a small circle out of the top centre of your biscuit whilst it is on the baking tray, roughly 5mm from the top by pressing a straw into the dough. This should lift out the perfect size of circle. When decorated, you can then thread some ribbon through the hole to make a hanging loop.

7. Put the shortbreads in the fridge to chill again for about 30 minutes.

8. Place in a pre-heated oven at 180°C for 8-12 minutes until they are starting to go golden around the edges.

9. Remove from the oven and place the biscuits on a wire rack to cool completely before icing.

Part Two: Making the icing:

1. Put the icing sugar and 70ml of the water in a large mixing bowl. Stir together with a metal spoon to stop the icing sugar from creating dust clouds when the electric whisk is introduced.

2. Now use the electric whisk to beat the icing sugar and water together for about 5 minutes. Add the remaining 10ml of water if the mixture is feeling too stiff / dry. The consistency should be like a thick, smooth paste.

3. Lay out the number of ramekins that correspond to the number of runny icing colours (the main biscuit coverage) that you will be using.

4. Take half to two thirds of the icing out of the bowl and divide it between the runny / flood icing ramekins.

5. Add a drop of each colour of food gel you want to use into each of these ramekins along with 1-5 teaspoons of cold water, which are added 1 teaspoon at a time and stirred into the icing to fully mix. You only add the teaspoons of water until a thick sauce consistency is achieved like a thick double cream.

6. Spoon each colour into a separate squeezy bottle and attach the nozzle to the top.

7. Now go back to the one third to half remaining thick icing in the large bowl. This can now be divided into ramekins, again using the number of ramekins that correspond to the number of colours of thick line icing you want to use.

8. Add a drop of food gel in the colours you want to use to each of the thick icing ramekins and stir until the food colouring is mixed in.

9. Now spoon each colour into a clean icing bag with writing nozzle fitted. You can rest each one in an empty mug for ease if you want. Fill the bag just over half full and push the icing down to the bottom. Twist the top of the bag and tie in a knot so that the icing doesn't come out of the top.

10. You are now ready to ice your biscuits!

Part Three: Icing the biscuits:

1. Take your first biscuit and the icing colour that you want to use for your outer edge line. This will be your thicker line icing in the bag.

Pipe a continuous line around the entire edge of the biscuit top making sure that no gaps are left.

2. Repeat for all the biscuits.

3. Take the colour that you want to use for the flood filling of your first biscuit. This will be your thinner icing in the squeezy bottles. Squeeze out enough icing so that it fills the section within the outer line icing. You can tilt the biscuit to ensure that it runs up against all the line icing.

4. Repeat in whichever flood colours you choose for all the remaining biscuits.

5. You can put a contrast flood colour on top of the main flood colour if you want, for example to create a spot design.

6. Leave the flood icing to dry.

7. You can put more thick line detail on top of the flood icing when it has dried to create details such as eyes or mouths on animal shaped biscuits, zig zags or bows on Easter egg biscuits etc.

8. Your biscuits are now complete. Leave them to dry thoroughly and then store in an airtight tin for up to 2 weeks.

Lemon Curd Pavlova

Granny Hooper was renowned for her pavlovas with their lovely mallow centres and crisp, golden outsides. Her signature one was a raspberry pavlova. She would make the meringue base a few days in advance and keep it stored in her oven until required. As a result, whenever we went to stay at her house, one of the first things we would do was rush into the kitchen and peep through the glass oven door to see whether there was a meringue base sitting in there. If there was, there would be great excitement as we knew we would be in for a dessert treat very soon!

This recipe has more Easter flavours with the use of the lemon curd. It is the same Granny Hooper meringue base, but the raspberry cream topping is replaced with a lemon curd cream topping and also the addition of some Easter egg decorations!

Serves 8 – 10

Lemon curd makes 2 small or 1 large jar and takes 30 minutes to prepare/cook

Meringue takes 20 minutes to prepare, 1 hour to cook, 15 minutes to assemble

Ingredients	Equipment
Lemon Curd • 4 large egg yolks • 200g caster sugar • 4 lemons, zest and juice • 100g salted butter cut into chunks Meringue base • 3 egg whites • 200g caster sugar • 1 teaspoon cornflour • 1 teaspoon vinegar • 1 teaspoon vanilla extract Decoration • Sugar coated chocolate mini eggs • 300ml double cream • 3 tablespoons of the lemon curd above will be used (or shop bought if you are not making your own) • Optional additional pouring cream or lemon curd to serve	• Medium sized Pyrex mixing bowl • Medium sized saucepan • Wooden spoon • Weighing scales • Knife • Juicer • Grater • Sterilised jam jars (2 small or 1 large) • Large very clean mixing bowl • Electric hand whisk • Balloon whisk, if you prefer to hand whip cream • Small bowl • Baking tray • Parchment paper • Pencil • Spatula • Serving dish / cake stand

Granny Hooper Tip:

To sterilise your jam jars for the lemon curd, run the jar and lid through the dishwasher or soak and wash with hot soapy water.

<u>Part One:</u> Lemon Curd

1. Half fill the saucepan with boiling water and place the Pyrex bowl on top. Put on the hob over a medium heat.

2. Put the lemon juice and zest as well as the sugar into the bowl and stir with the wooden spoon.

3. When the sugar has all dissolved, turn the heat down to low and slowly add the egg yolks, making sure that you stir continuously to avoid the yolks cooking as lumps.

4. Now add the chunks of butter – these will create a lovely sheen to the curd.

5. When the butter is all melted, turn the heat up and continue to cook for a further 10 minutes, stirring slowly all the time. You will feel it thickening.

6. Once the time is up, turn off the heat and lift the bowl off the pan. Let the bowl cool to almost room temperature. If the curd did not thicken, then remove the water from the pan and pour the curd from the bowl into the pan. Cook on a medium heat stirring all the time until it does thicken. It will still be quite runny as it thickens more when cool. It should be like thick cream.

7. When sufficiently cool, spoon the curd into the sterilised jars. Put the lids on and place in the fridge. Consume within 1 month.

Part Two: Make the Pavlova

1. In a very clean bowl, whisk the egg whites until stiff by not dry.

2. Mix the cornflour, vinegar and vanilla together in a small bowl and whisk into the egg whites.

3. Add the sugar and whisk until the mixture is heavy and smooth. It should have a silky gloss to it.

4. Take a baking tray and a piece of parchment paper about the size of the tray. Now dollop a coin-sized amount of the meringue mix onto each corner of the tray and place the parchment paper on top. Press the paper onto each corner dollop and the meringue will stick the paper to the tray like glue.

5. Draw a rough circle in pencil on the parchment paper making it slightly smaller than your proposed serving dish. This will act as a guide when creating your meringue base.

6. Use the spatula to scoop out the meringue mixture from the bowl and then spread it in a circular shape approximately 3-5cm deep, ready for cooking.

Granny Hooper Tip:

Granny Hooper would make her meringue base rustic in appearance, so she would use the tip of the spatula to create swirls in the meringue. She would also build up the edges slightly so that they would create a wall to contain the filling inside.

7. Place in the oven at 130°C and bake for 1 hour.

Granny Hooper Tip:

When the cooking time is complete, make sure you turn off the oven, but leave the meringue inside until it is completely cool – ideally overnight. If you take it out early or cook it on a higher heat the meringue will deflate.

Part Three: Decorate the Pavlova

You should assemble your pavlova no more than 1-2 hours before serving to ensure that the meringue stays nice and crunchy on the outside.

1. Take your meringue base off the parchment paper and place it in the centre of your serving dish or cake stand.

2. Whip your cream using a balloon whisk or electric whisk until soft peaks are formed. Take care not to overwhip.

3. Take 3 tablespoons of lemon curd and gently fold it through the whipped cream using a metal spoon. Try to not mix it too much as you want to have a rippled effect which is both attractive to look at and also tastes nice, having the contrast of the different intense lemon and the cream sections.

4. Spoon the lemon cream onto the top of the meringue base keeping it within the centre section, so that the outer meringue wall is on display. You can keep the lemon cream in rustic dollops to preserve the ripple effect rather than smoothing it completely flat.

5. Drop your sugar-coated chocolate eggs randomly over the top of the lemon cream so that each slice should receive 3 or 4.

6. Your impressive pavlova is now ready to serve on dessert plates with spoons and forks. It can be served on its own or with some additional pouring cream or lemon curd on the side.

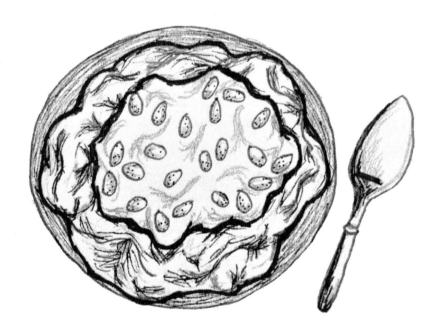

Easter Biscuits

Granny Hooper would call these Easter Cakes, but they are actually more like biscuits, so I have altered the name slightly. Part of the recipe requires the mixture to chill for a few hours, so please bear this in mind when you are planning your bake.

Makes 18-20 biscuits

Preparation time 20 minutes with 2-3 hours chilling time. Cooking time 10-15 minutes.

Ingredients	Equipment
• 300g plain flour • 225g salted butter • 110g caster sugar • 2 egg yolks • 50g currants • Two strands of saffron • 1 dessert spoon of brandy	• large mixing bowl • 78mm fluted pastry cutter • Rolling pin • Wooden spoon • Dessertspoon • Sieve • Wire rack • Cling film or beeswax wrap • Palette Knife • Weighing scales • Teacup • Non-stick baking tray

1. Put the brandy and saffron in the teacup and stir until the saffron has infused in the brandy. Now remove the saffron strands so that the coloured brandy remains.

2. Cream the butter and sugar together in the mixing bowl.

3. Add the egg yolks and brandy and mix well.

4. Sieve in the flour and combine until a paste is formed.

5. Cover the bowl with cling film or beeswax and leave to cool in the fridge for 2-3 hours.

6. Dust a worksurface with flour and roll the chilled mixture until it is around 3mm thick.

7. Use the pastry cutter to cut out as many biscuits as you can from the mixture, re-rolling any offcuts until it is all used up.

8. Use the palette knife to lift each biscuit onto a non-stick baking tray.

9. Bake at 180°C for 10-15 minutes until the biscuits are starting to go light brown around the edges.

10. Remove and cool on the wire rack.

11. Store in an airtight tin for around a week.

Chocolate Nests
Makes about 10

Takes about 20 minutes to prepare and 1 hour to set

Ingredients	Equipment
• 200g milk chocolate • 50g salted butter cubed • 2½ tablespoons golden syrup • 5 bars of shredded wheat crushed • 1 tube or large bag of sugar-coated mini eggs	• medium sized Pyrex mixing bowl • medium sized saucepan • wooden spoon • metal dessert spoon • tablespoon • metal cupcake or bun tray • weighing scales • cupcake cases

1. Fill the saucepan half full with boiling water and place on the hob. Place the Pyrex bowl on top of the saucepan.

2. Break the chocolate into the bowl and add the butter and golden syrup.

3. Stir with the wooden spoon until all the ingredients have melted to liquid form and mixed together.

4. Turn off the heat and take the bowl off the saucepan.

5. Crumble the shredded wheat into the chocolate mix and stir until it is all fully coated.

6. Put the cupcake cases into the bun tray holes.

7. Use the dessert spoon to fill each cupcake case with the chocolate coated shredded wheat mixture. Use the spoon to press the mixture firmly into a nest shape. It will set slightly, so by compacting it, it will help prevent it from crumbling when eating.

8. When the tray is filled, decorate each nest with 3 sugar-coated mini eggs, using a selection of colours in each one.

9. Place in the fridge to set slightly for about 1 hour, then transfer to an airtight tin until they are ready to be eaten.

Hot Cross Buns

Hot Cross Buns are delicious sweet, spiced, fruit buns with a bread-like texture and a white cross on the top. They are traditionally eaten on Good Friday, but nowadays tend to be eaten any time in the run up to Easter. The cross on the top represents Jesus being crucified on the cross and the spices symbolise the spices that were used to embalm him at his burial. They even have a traditional nursery rhyme written about them, "Hot cross buns, hot cross buns, one a penny, two a penny, hot cross buns". The composer appears to be unknown, but it is believed to have started as a cry from bakers as early as the 1700s, calling out to their customers about what they were selling.

Granny Hooper Tradition:

I remember Granny Hooper toasting hot cross buns in her wire toasting rack on the boiling plate of her Aga and serving, cut in half and buttered, with a cup of tea at tea-time.

My mother replicates this by toasting hers under the grill on her oven. The cut side faces up to the grill and has a lovely crunchy texture to it, but you do have to keep an eye on them as they burn very easily. I am rather lazy and just pop mine in the toaster. The result isn't quite as nice, but for speed and ease it is good enough!

Serves 12

Preparation 40 minutes, Rising time 3 hours, Baking 20 minutes

Ingredients	Equipment
Buns	• Two large mixing bowls
• 110g caster sugar	• Cling film or beeswax wrap
• 10g instant dried yeast	• Weighing scales
• 640g strong white bread flour (plus extra for dusting)	• Baking tray
	• Parchment paper
• 375ml warm milk	• Wooden spoon
• 50g melted salted butter (plus extra for greasing)	• Teaspoon
	• Plastic bag large enough to contain the baking tray
• 2 teaspoons cinnamon	• Small bowl
• 2 teaspoons all spice	• Disposable piping bag
• 150g sultanas	• Scissors
• 50g chopped mixed peel	• Wire rack
• 2 oranges, zest only	• Small saucepan
• 1 egg	• Pastry brush
Crosses	• Sieve
• 75g plain white flour	
• 75ml water	
Glaze	
• 75g melted, sieved apricot jam	

1. Place the flour, sugar, spices, orange zest and yeast in the mixing bowl and stir together.

2. Make a well (hole) in the middle of the mixture and put in the egg, butter and milk. Stir, bringing the flour mixture in from the sides gradually until it is all combined to form a soft dough.

3. Use your hands to take the dough off the spoon and the edges of the bowl.

4. Dust the worksurface with flour and put the dough onto it.

5. Start to knead the dough with your hands, pushing the dough away from you with the base of your palm and folding it back over itself before pulling it back again. Repeat this process continually for 10 minutes until the dough is no longer sticky, but soft and smooth.

6. Put the sultanas and mixed peel onto the dough and wrap the dough around them to form a ball.

7. Knead the ball until the fruit is evenly distributed within the dough.

8. Grease a large mixing bowl and place the dough inside. Cover it with the cling film or beeswax wrap and place it somewhere warm for about 2 hours until it has risen to double the size.

9. Flour the worksurface again and spread out the dough onto it.

10. Knead the dough for a further 5-10 minutes and then place back in the mixing bowl with the cling film or beeswax wrap on top to rise for another hour.

11. Punch all the air out of the dough and divide it into 12. Roll each piece into a ball and place on a baking tray lined with baking parchment. The balls should be placed in a 3 x 4 ball grid.

12. Put the tray inside the plastic bag and seal the end. Leave in a warm place for about an hour to double in size again. It doesn't matter if they are touching each other when they have risen, as they are usually torn apart when bought from a bakery.

13. In a small bowl, mix the plain flour and water together then pour into a disposable piping bag. Cut off the end to give a 5mm opening.

14. Pipe crosses on the top of all the buns.

15. Preheat the oven to 220°C.

16. Bake in the oven for 20 minutes until they are light brown in colour.

17. Remove from the oven and put on a wire rack.

18. Warm the apricot jam and water in a small saucepan and then sieve.

19. Use the pastry brush to lightly glaze the tops of the buns and give them a lovely glaze.

20. Let the buns cool thoroughly on the wire rack otherwise they will not hold their shape when you cut them.

21. Serve sliced in half and toasted with butter, as detailed above.

Easter Cake

My mother usually serves a light orange sponge cake for tea on Easter Day instead of the slightly richer Simnel Cake. Both types of cake are delicious, so I have included the two options so that you can try them both. This cake is probably more appealing to young children than the Simnel Cake as it is usually decorated with sugar-coated chocolate mini eggs and little Easter decorations, which make it very attractive.

For the decorations, we used to have small ceramic ornaments of rabbits and chicks which could be reused each year. Easter decorations are becoming more popular, so a wide range should be available in shops or online for you to choose from.

Serves 10-12

Preparation 20-30 minutes, Baking 20 minutes

Ingredients	Equipment
• 225g salted butter	• large mixing bowl
• 225g caster sugar	• Two 20cm diameter non-stick cake tins
• 4 large eggs	(loose bottomed is preferable)
• 225g self-raising flour	• Weighing scales
• 1 teaspoon baking powder	• Juicer
• Zest and juice of 1 orange (1	• Grater
tablespoon of juice for the cake	• Wooden spoon
mixture, the rest for the icing)	• Teaspoon
• 300g regular icing sugar	• Metal tablespoon
• 3 tablespoons lemon curd (shop-	• Sieve
bought or the recipe earlier in this	• Easter cake decorations
book)	• Baking parchment
• 1 bag of sugar-coated chocolate	• Pencil
mini eggs	• Scissors
	• Wire rack
	• Metal skewer
	• Palette knife
	• Small mixing bowl

1. Place the butter and caster sugar in the mixing bowl and beat together with the wooden spoon until a light creamy texture has been achieved.

2. Crack the eggs into the mix one at a time, stirring each one in fully before adding the next. If you add the eggs all at once, the mixture is likely to curdle.

3. Add the orange zest and stir in thoroughly.

4. Sieve the flour and baking powder into the bowl with the metal spoon.

5. Stir the flour into the mixture carefully with the metal spoon until it is all combined. This is called folding. You must do it in as few stirs as

you can, as the more you stir after adding the flour, the less the cake will rise.

6. Add the orange juice a teaspoon at a time until the mixture loosens slightly, but is still quite thick like a heavy batter.

7. Preheat the oven to 180°C.

8. Place the cake tins on the baking parchment and draw around them using the pencil. Cut out the circles and place one in the bottom of each non-stick cake tin.

9. Divide the cake mixture between the two tins and use the back of the spoon to gently spread the mixture to ensure it is evenly distributed in the tin, but without pushing it down too much or it will restrict the rise.

10. Place the tins on the middle shelf of the oven and bake for 20 minutes.

11. Check that you don't have any doors or windows open that would create a sudden cool breeze for the cakes. Now take the cakes out of the oven and place a metal skewer in the centre of each. If it comes out clean, the cake is ready. If not, return to the oven for a further 2-3 minutes.

12. Once cooked, remove the cakes from the oven, but leave in their tins for 5 minutes so as not to rapidly reduce their temperature.

13. Now push up the base of the tin to remove each cake and place it on the wire rack to cool thoroughly.

14. Once cool, remove the parchment paper circles from the base of each cake.

15. Take the plate that you want to serve the cake on and place one of the two cakes onto the plate. The top of the cake should be the side that is touching the plate and the side of the cake that you peeled the parchment paper from should be facing upwards.

16. Spread the lemon curd on the upwards facing side of the cake using the palette knife.

17. Take the second cake and place the side which you peeled the parchment paper from so that it is touching the lemon curd on the cake that is already on the serving plate.

18. Your cake is now ready to ice.

19. In the small mixing bowl, sieve the icing sugar and add ½ tablespoon of orange juice. Stir until the icing sugar and juice are mixed with no lumps, adding more juice as required.

20. When a consistency of pouring cream is achieved, you can pour some of the icing onto the top of the cake.

21. Pour some very hot water onto the palette knife to warm it, then use it to spread the icing on the top of the cake. The heat from the knife should give the icing a smooth, shiny finish. Add more icing if required until a good coverage is achieved, but it is not dripping down the sides.

22. You can place any ceramic or plastic decorations on top of the cake now in a design of your choice.

23. Leave the cake to harden for a few hours.

24. Once the icing on the top has hardened slightly, you can place the sugar-coated chocolate eggs on the top of the cake too.

Granny Hooper Tip:

Do not be tempted to place the sugar-coated eggs on top of the cake before the icing has hardened slightly as there will be too much liquid still remaining in the icing and it will make the colour bleed from the eggs. This will make them look unappetising.

Chapter 4, Easter Weekend:

Maundy Thursday

Maundy Thursday is the fifth day of Holy Week and commemorates the Last Supper for Jesus with his disciples and the evening that Jesus was betrayed by Judas in the Garden of Gethsemane.

Tradition:

In England, Royal Maundy is a religious service where the monarch gives out small silver coins called "Maundy Money". These days they are given to people over the age of 70 in recognition for their contributions to the church or their community. The Maundy coins are rare, so they are very valuable.

Good Friday and Fish Pie

In England, Good Friday is a national holiday.

Tradition:

Good Friday is the day that Jesus died. It is believed that a way to recognise his sacrifice, was for Christians to fast on this day. It was however acceptable for fish to be eaten on a fasting day, which is why fish tends to be eaten on Fridays and particularly on Good Friday.

There are many fish dishes that can be served on Good Friday, but a couple of my favourite options are either poached salmon or fish pie. Granny Hooper used to make a beautiful poached salmon which was slowly poached in the coolest oven of her Aga. This was then served with boiled, buttered, new potatoes and green vegetables. Another fish dish that she regularly served was her fish pie. This had a lovely crunchy cheese topping that sat on the creamy mashed potato and mixed fish below.

I have to confess that there was one ingredient in her fish pie that I really did not like, and that was the eggs. I therefore never include them when I make her fish pie, but I have added them as an optional ingredient in the recipe below!

Granny Hooper's Fish Pie:

Serves 4-6

Preparation: 40 minutes, Cooking: 20-30 minutes

Ingredients	Equipment

White sauce:
  • 50g salted butter
  • 50g plain flour
  • 568ml milk
  • Pepper
 	
Fish pie mixture:
  • 200g smoked haddock chunks
  • 250g salmon chunks
  • 250g cod or haddock chunks
  • 100g uncooked shelled prawns
  • 1 tablespoon chopped parsley
  • 100g frozen peas
  • Optional 2 hard-boiled eggs, shelled and chopped
 	
Mashed potato:
  • 350g potatoes, peeled and halved
  • 20ml milk
  • 20g salted butter
  • Pepper
 	
Garnish:
  • 50g mature Cheddar cheese, grated
	• Two large saucepans
	• Sauce beater
	• Weighing scales
	• Tablespoon
	• Grater
	• Knife
	• Chopping board
	• Potato masher
	• Ceramic or Pyrex serving dish approximately 30cm x 20cm

Part One: White Sauce

1. Place the butter in a large saucepan and heat on the hob until melted.

2. Add the flour a tablespoon at a time, stirring with the sauce beater after each addition. When it is all added, cook through for a minute.

3. Slowly pour in the milk. Use the sauce beater to combine the milk with the flour mix. By adding the milk slowly, you will ensure a lump-free sauce is achieved.

4. Grind in some black pepper to season and stir to combine this.

Part Two: Fish Pie Mix

1. Add the smoked fish, salmon and unsmoked fish chunks to the white sauce. Stir in gently with the wooden spoon and then leave to cook through gently on a low heat for about 3-4 minutes.

2. Add the frozen peas and prawns. Stir gently to give an even distribution, but being careful not break up the chunks of fish.

3. When the prawns turn pink, turn off the heat and add the chopped parsley. If you are adding hard boiled eggs, you would add these now. Stir through to mix everything evenly.

4. Spoon the fish pie mix into the Pyrex dish and leave to cool slightly.

Part Three: Mashed Potato

1. Place the peeled, chopped potatoes in a large pan of boiling water.

2. Boil on the hob for 20 minutes until you can easily stick a knife into them, but not so much that they are disintegrating in the water.

3. Drain the potatoes and put the butter in the pan with them. Put the lid on the saucepan and let the heat from the potatoes melt the butter slightly.

4. Use the potato masher to mash the potatoes until there are no lumps remaining.

5. Now add the milk a little at a time, mashing after each addition until a smooth, creamy mash is achieved. Do not use all the milk if the mash is starting to go too runny. It should be able to hold a good shape.

6. Grind in some black pepper to season and stir to combine this.

7. Spoon the mashed potato over the fish pie mix and use the back of a fork to gently spread it around the dish to ensure an even layer all over the top of the fish pie mix. The fork can also be used to create a stripy pattern on the top. This will look attractive when it is cooked.

8. Preheat the oven at 180°C.

9. Finally sprinkle the grated cheese over the top of the mashed potato and put in the oven for 20-30 minutes until the top is golden and you can see the fish pie sauce bubbling underneath.

10. Serve with mixed vegetables such as broccoli and carrots.

Granny Hooper Tip:

If you want to prepare your fish pie in advance, you can complete all the stages up to the stage where you are about to place the finished pie in the oven, then place in the fridge if you will be using within 24 hours, or cover with a lid or freezer-proof wrap if you want to freeze. If freezing, ensure the pie is fully defrosted before placing in the oven to cook.

Tea-time on Good Friday:

A tea-time treat particularly associated with Good Friday is Hot Cross Buns. The recipe is featured in Chapter 3 of this book. The infamous cross on the top of each bun symbolises the cross on which Jesus was crucified.

Easter Sunday

Easter Sunday is the day where Christians celebrate the resurrection of Jesus.

In England, extended families will often gather together on Easter Sunday to celebrate together. There is usually an Easter Sunday lunch which, for meat-eaters, will consist of roast lamb, served with spring vegetables, roast potatoes, gravy and redcurrant jelly. The reason that lamb is chosen is because it symbolises Jesus being a human sacrifice.

The Easter lunch is a special meal, so it is nice to make an effort with your table decorations. Like Granny Hooper, my mother always creates an attractive table for our lunch on this day. She will use a spring-coloured tablecloth as the base, for example a fresh shade of green and Easter decorative paper napkins, which are widely available in supermarkets and gift shops at this time of year. She might use a flower arrangement like the one described in Chapter 2 as a centre-piece for the table along with some spring-yellow tall candles and little Easter ornaments such as ceramic chicks and rabbits. Also, small dishes containing sugar coated chocolate eggs are positioned randomly around the centre of the table.

At each place setting there will be a large Easter egg with an envelope or present addressed to the person to be seated at that place. The envelopes are usually for the adults and contain a gift of Easter money. The gifts are usually for the children.

Once the roast lamb has been enjoyed, a dessert such as the Lemon Curd Pavlova from Chapter 3 will be served.

If you plan to serve wine, reds normally accompany roast lamb. Good matches would be Pinot Noir, Fleurie, Rioja, Medoc or Merlot. If you prefer white, consider White Rioja or a lightly oaked Chardonnay.

Tradition:

A popular Easter Day activity is to hold an Easter egg hunt in the garden. Although this tradition is usually for children only, in our family the adults take part as well.

Granny Hooper used to have a lovely big garden with numerous hiding places, so it was very easy to hold a hunt for aunts, uncles, cousins etc. with hundreds of eggs being hidden. The Easter Bunny is supposed to hide the foil-wrapped, small, chocolate eggs for children to find and collect in baskets or small bags.

In our family, the host of Easter Day will have bought several bags of different colour foil-wrapped eggs that are sold in shops from as early as January! Traditionally these eggs were solid chocolate, but now the chocolatiers produce them with centres including caramel, praline and mint, to name but a few.

The host will open all the bags and write a list detailing how many eggs there are with each wrapper design. These will then be divided between those that are hunting the eggs and a list will be written for each hunter. For example, 3 red eggs, 2 green eggs, 7 pink eggs, 4 blue eggs etc. The host will find an opportunity when the lunch guests are occupied and will sneak into the garden to hide the eggs in places such as on plant pots, window sills, tree branches, on fence posts etc.

Once hidden, the host will summon all the family members and issue them each with a paper bag and list of eggs to find. Everyone then goes into the garden to hunt for their rations! The children often rush around the garden trying to find the eggs as quickly as they can and it is usually the adults who are slow to find their quota. In our family, Grandpa usually needs the grandchildren to help him find his!

After the excitement of the egg hunt, everyone is usually ready for a cup of tea. This will be served with either a Simnel Cake or Easter Cake, Easter biscuits and possibly more Hot Cross Buns. Recipes for all of these are given in Chapter 3.

The day after Easter Sunday is known in England as Easter Monday. It is a national holiday although no specific traditions take place on this day, so our Easter celebrations stop on this day. We continue to enjoy the decorations we have put up around the house for another week or so, then take them down until the next Easter.

Acknowledgements

I would like to thank my grandmother, Granny Hooper, for teaching me how to cook, bake and craft as well as passing on the family traditions that surround many of the annual celebrations in the English calendar. You are the inspiration for all the content within the Granny Hooper ™ brand.

I would also like to thank my parents for their continued support and advice whilst writing this publication and other material within the brand. My mother for being my editor in chief and my father for being my technical advisor!

I thank my husband and daughters for being my food samplers and crafting assistants.

Printed in Great Britain
by Amazon